BOOK CHARGING CARD

973
SAN

34880049985125

Accession No. _____   Call No. dup

Author Sandler, Martin

Title America's Great Disasters

Date Loaned	Borrower's Name	Date Returned

BAKER & TAYLOR

AMERICA'S GREAT DISASTERS

by

Martin W. Sandler

HARPERCOLLINS*PUBLISHERS*

For Carol, who makes it all happen
—M.S.

ACKNOWLEDGMENTS

I wish to thank Craig R. Sandler for his inspired research help. I am also most appreciative of the aid I received from Kate Riley and Lisa Hinzman of the State Historical Society of Wisconsin; Anna Pebler of Galveston's Rosenberg Library; Nicole Weld and Eleanor Gillers of the New-York Historical Society; Robin Rummel of the Johnstown Flood Museum; and Jesse Johnson of the Library of Congress. Finally, I am most grateful to Sarah Thomson and Mark McVeigh, my editors. Their suggestions and help in shaping this book go far beyond their acknowledged editing skills.

America's Great Disasters   Copyright © 2003 by Martin Sandler
All rights reserved. No part of this book may be used or reproduced in any manner whatsoever without written permission except in the case of brief quotations embodied in critical articles and reviews.
Manufactured in China.
For information address HarperCollins Children's Books, a division of HarperCollins Publishers
1350 Avenue of the Americas, New York, NY 10019.
www.harperchildrens.com

Library of Congress Cataloging-in-Publication Data
Sandler, Martin.
America's great disasters / by Martin Sandler.
p. cm.
Summary: Examines the causes and effects of such American disasters as the sinking of the steamboat *Sultana* in 1871, the Johnstown flood, the Dust Bowl, and the influenza epidemic of 1918–19.
ISBN 0-06-029107-9 — ISBN 0-06-029108-7 (lib. bdg.)
1. Disasters—United States—History—Anecdotes—Juvenile literature.
2. United States—History—Anecdotes—Juvenile literature. [1. Disasters.] I. Title.
E179.S217 2002   2001039218
973—dc21   CIP
AC

Typography by Carla Weise
2 3 4 5 6 7 8 9 10
❖
First Edition

CONTENTS

People throughout the world know the sad tale of the 1912 sinking of the luxury liner *Titanic*, in which 1,513 passengers were killed. But the *Titanic* sinking was not the most devastating of all maritime disasters.

DISASTERS AT SEA

Disaster at sea! From the days of tall-masted, canvas-laden sailing vessels through the golden age of luxury liners, the sea has been the site of disasters far too numerous to count.

Sailing vessels were always vulnerable to unexpected storms with mast-splintering winds and waves big enough to swamp or capsize even the largest of ships. When steam replaced wind as the most common means of propelling vessels, a new kind of danger was introduced: Tens of thousands of travelers and crewmen lost their lives when the boilers that supplied the steam exploded, tearing vessels apart and turning what was left of them into raging infernos.

Even when ships became safer, they were still vulnerable to human error. Many tragedies were caused by captains and navigators who miscalculated where they were or where they were heading and collided with other ships or crashed their vessels onto rocks, reefs, or unfamiliar coastlines.

The most famous of all disasters at sea involved the 46,500-ton luxury liner *Titanic*. On its 1912 maiden voyage from England to the United States, the supposedly unsinkable vessel struck an iceberg and sank; 1,513 people lost their lives.

Many people today still believe that the sinking of the *Titanic* was the maritime disaster in which the largest number of American lives were lost. But that dubious honor belongs to another vessel.

THE SULTANA EXPLOSION

The American Civil War claimed more than six hundred thousand American lives and left hundreds of thousands terribly wounded. Before the four-year conflict finally ended in April 1865, much of the southern half of the nation lay in ruins.

By the time the Southern (Confederate) army led by General Robert E. Lee finally surrendered to the Northern (Union) forces headed by General Ulysses S. Grant, thousands of Union soldiers were being held captive under terrible conditions in Confederate prisons.

Even before the official surrender took place, it became obvious that the end of the war was near. Confederate officials began to make arrangements to exchange Union prisoners for the Confederate prisoners held in Union camps in the North. It was decided that Union captives held in two of the worst Southern prisons, Andersonville and Cahaba, would be transported to the southern port of Vicksburg, Mississippi. From there the prisoners would be taken by steamboats up the Mississippi River to freedom in the North. "Glad shouts of joy rent the air, when the news [of our release] came to us," stated Union private George Schmutz. "We were soldiers, prisoners of war, who had been shut up in prison pens, some for six months, some for twelve, some for eighteen months. One might think how glad all were to get home."

By the second week of April 1865, thousands of Union prisoners were in Vicksburg, ready to board the steamboats that would take them north. One of the largest of these vessels was the 260-foot *Sultana*, built almost entirely of wood. Captained and partly owned by J. Cass Mason, the *Sultana* had been constructed to carry 376 passengers.

But the *Sultana*'s captain was aware that the military was paying five dollars for every soldier and ten dollars for every officer loaded onto a ship. Having befriended officials overseeing the loading operations, Mason convinced them that the *Sultana* could transport far more passengers than she was supposed to carry. In the confusion of loading so many prisoners onto the various vessels, the officials failed to keep accurate records and had no idea of just how many people Mason was cramming aboard his ship.

The soldiers were not the only ones to climb aboard. Some hundred civilians, including several women, asked Captain Mason if they could book passage on his ship. Mason quickly agreed. And as if the human cargo was not enough, Mason arranged to make even more money on the voyage by filling the hold with 250 heavy barrels of sugar and 97 cases of wine. He also loaded some hundred mules and horses and an equal number of hogs onto the main deck at the very rear of the ship.

On April 24, Captain Mason decided that he had packed every last passenger and piece of cargo he could fit onto his ship. At nine o'clock that evening, the *Sultana* pulled out of the dock at Vicksburg and began its journey to Cairo, Illinois. "[When] we arrive safely in Cairo," the ship's chief clerk, William Gambrel, told one of the soldiers on board, "it will be the greatest trip ever made on the western waters, as there are more people on board than were ever carried on one boat on the Mississippi River." Asked to estimate just how many people were aboard the vessel, Gambrel replied, "Twenty-four hundred soldiers, one hundred citizen-passengers and a crew of about eighty—in all, over twenty-five hundred!" This on a ship built to carry 376.

As the *Sultana* made its way up the Mississippi, crew members continually warned the passengers that if too many of them shifted from one side of the vessel to the other, the ship would be in real danger of capsizing. What the passengers didn't know was that the *Sultana* had experienced serious trouble with all four of her boilers in the previous few months. Her engineers had actually repaired a rupture in one boiler with a temporary patch.

Three days out of Vicksburg, while the steamboat was in mid-river within sight of Memphis, Tennessee, disaster struck. At two o'clock in the morning, and without any warning, the *Sultana*'s boilers exploded. "[The] explosion came with a [noise] exceeding any artillery I had ever heard," recalled Private Benjamin Johnson, "and I had heard some that were very heavy, especially at Gettysburg." Months later, Johnson's fellow soldier Arthur Jones would describe the blast even more dramatically. "What a crash," wrote Jones. "Such hissing of steam, the crash of the different decks . . . the falling of the massive smoke stacks . . . We had faced death day by day . . . , but this was far more appalling than any scene through which we had passed."

The explosion hurled hundreds of passengers high into the air, dropping them back on the deck or into the Mississippi. Just as quickly, the *Sultana* burst into flames. "The fire shot up and I saw sights so terrible and heart-rending I fail to have language to explain," recalled soldier Andrew Perry. "The lower deck . . . was covered with the dead and wounded. Some were scalded, some seemed to be blind, some of them would rise up partly and fall, and some were pinned down with the timbers of the wreck. I saw hundreds in this frightful plight, crying, praying, screaming, begging, groaning, and moaning."

When the *Sultana*'s boilers exploded, most passengers were either killed or hurled into the river. "The wildest confusion followed," recalled one survivor. "I could hear the groans of the dying above the flames."

Most of those who died were soldiers. After surviving bloody battles like Shiloh, Antietam, and Gettysburg, enduring months of inadequate food and harsh treatment in the prison camps, they were simply not strong enough to avoid the fires or dig themselves out of the wreckage before the ship sank. Hundreds of others jumped or were thrown into the river by the

THE GENERAL SLOCUM

Because it was so vastly unreported, the *Sultana* tragedy did not lead to a public outcry. Thirty-nine years later, however, another great steamboat catastrophe made the front pages of all the nation's newspapers and led to the most sweeping maritime reforms in United States history.

On June 15, 1904, 1,306 children, teachers, and chaperones, all members of a New York City church, climbed aboard the steamboat *General Slocum* and headed for a picnic on a point of land a few miles outside of New York Harbor. The *General Slocum* was terribly overloaded. It should have been carrying fewer than half the number of people who were aboard.

And in violation of all safety regulations, a storeroom on board was filled with cans of oil and barrels of highly flammable material.

Shortly after the vessel left its pier, the oil was set afire when a crew member lit a lamp and carelessly tossed the match aside. Soon a fourteen-year old passenger saw smoke coming from the storeroom. Pushing his way through the crowded deck, the boy found the steamboat's captain and told him what he had seen. The captain paid no attention to the boy, telling him "to mind your own business."

Within minutes the *General Slocum* was fully ablaze. When crewmembers attempted to fight the fire, they found that the ship's

blast but then drowned because, like most Americans of the time, they did not know how to swim. Beaches, pools, and swimming itself did not become popular until very late in the 1800s.

A few passengers managed to survive the initial blast. One of them, Alexander Brown, found himself floating down the river. After drifting for several miles, he bumped into a partly submerged small island in the middle of the river and managed to climb into a tree that was growing there. During the four hours he spent in the tree before being saved, Brown learned a lesson that would stay with him for the rest of his life. "Now," he later wrote, "when I hear persons talking about being hard up, I think of my condition at hoses did not work. Panicked passengers discovered the vessel's ten lifeboats could not be used. Some had been lashed so tightly together that they could not be dislodged. Others could not be budged because they were stuck together by a thick coat of paint. The life preservers aboard the vessel were much too heavy, so the children who managed to strap them on were pulled straight down to the bottom of the harbor. By the time the *General Slocum* had crashed onto a rock and fireboats had finally arrived to put out the blaze, 1,031 people, mostly children, were dead.

Following an inquiry that revealed the inexcusable negligence that had caused the disaster, a shocked nation demanded that changes be made. Laws were passed regulating the number of passengers an excursion vessel could carry, the ways in which lifeboats had to be tied to the deck, and the construction of life preservers. Other laws banned the transport of hazardous materials on passenger ships and called for complete inspection before a ship was allowed to leave dock. They were all important, far-reaching regulations. But for the innocent victims of the *General Slocum*, they came too late.

that time—up in a tree in the middle of the Mississippi River, a thousand miles from home, not one cent to my name, nor a pocket to put it in."

Not everyone on the *Sultana* concentrated on saving themselves. When the explosion occurred, soldier William Shummard, like most of the passengers, was asleep. Rudely awakened by the blast, he was lucky enough to find a life preserver lying next to him. Just as he was putting it on, however, he noticed a terrified young girl preparing to jump into the river. Aware that her chances for survival were slim, Shummard took the life preserver and fastened it around her. His unselfish act enabled the girl to stay afloat in the river until she was rescued. Shummard was also one of the fortunate ones. By grabbing onto a piece of wreckage he was able to make his way safely to the riverbank.

Although his greed in outrageously overloading his ship was a major factor in the disaster, Captain Mason performed heroically once the blast occurred. Rather than leaving the vessel, he devoted himself to pulling injured passengers from the fallen and burning wreckage. Before the *Sultana* sank, Mason handed out as many doors, chairs, and any other pieces of debris as he could for passengers to cling to once they were in the river.

The people of Memphis did whatever they could to aid the *Sultana*. Many set out in rowboats and sailboats and plucked people out of the water. Other citizens built fires along the Memphis wharf to guide survivors to shore.

When daylight finally dawned, the scene was appalling. Bodies continued to float down the river. Dozens of survivors, like Alexander Brown, remained perched in trees along the riverbank across from Memphis and beyond. Many of the victims' bodies would never be found. Among the missing was Captain Mason.

Because of the inadequate records kept at the *Sultana*'s boarding in Vicksburg, exactly how many people died in the disaster will never be known. Estimates range from twenty-three hundred to almost three thousand. In May and June of 1865 an official government inquiry into the tragedy was held. Although dozens of witnesses were called to testify, ultimately no individual was found guilty of wrongdoing.

Despite its enormity, the tragedy received little attention in the nation's newspapers. The sinking of the *Sultana* occurred in the same month that the long and bitter Civil War finally ended. Day after day, the pages of the newspapers were filled with stories relating to the end of hostilities. Then, shortly after the war concluded, Abraham Lincoln was assassinated. Now the papers were filled from front to back with accounts of the assassination

Each year after the *Sultana* tragedy, its survivors held an emotional reunion. They shared the common bond of having lived through the greatest maritime disaster in the nation's history.

and the capture of the president's killer. No one had any attention to spare for the *Sultana*.

Soon after the *Sultana* disaster, the *Memphis Argus*, one of the few newspapers to pay attention to the event, stated, "We have, as a people, become so accustomed to the suffering of horrors during the past few years that they soon seem to lose their appalling features, and are forgotten. Only a few days ago [some twenty-five hundred] lives were sacrificed to fire and water, almost within sight of the city. Yet, even now the disaster is scarcely mentioned. . . ." Today, more than 135 years after the *Sultana* and its passengers met their fate, it remains America's greatest maritime disaster.

Floods have ranked among the world's greatest disasters since Biblical times. Here a citizen of Johnstown, Pennsylvania, views the aftermath of the United States's most tragic flood.

FLOOD:
Rising Waters

Mankind has been plagued by floods ever since human beings first walked the earth. The myths, legends, and writings of the Greeks, Egyptians, Persians, and other early civilizations are filled with accounts of ancient floods and the ways in which both gods and humans attempted to cope with them.

The United States, like almost every other nation, has experienced many floods. Those communities that lie along the banks of mighty rivers have been the hardest hit. In the fall of 1992 through the summer of 1993, a series of unusually heavy rains caused water levels along a thousand-mile stretch of the Mississippi River to reach record heights. By July 1993, with the heavy rains continuing, the Mississippi and the many rivers that feed into it began overflowing. The floodwaters poured into cities and farms along the riverbanks—killing fifty people, leaving seventy thousand homeless, and causing more than twelve billion dollars in damage.

Like this 1993 disaster, most floods are the result of nature in the form of record rainfall, melting snows, or hurricanes and other kinds of storms. But the most devastating flood ever to strike the United States was caused only in part by nature. The main reason for this disaster was human greed and neglect.

THE JOHNSTOWN FLOOD

In 1889 Johnstown, Pennsylvania, was one of the most important cities in America. Located in a valley between two rivers, it had long been a vital transportation center. More important, the rich deposits of iron ore that lay in the soil for miles around it had made Johnstown the largest steel-producing city in the nation.

And it was booming. New iron and steel factories were being built. Every day, it seemed, new people arrived to work in the factories. Newcomers were astounded to find that, unlike most cities of the day, Johnstown's streets were paved and many of its homes had electric lights, indoor plumbing, and telephones. The city's newest hotel even had an elevator.

The mountains surrounding Johnstown were lovely, filled with lush forests and all types of wildlife. One mountain area, fourteen miles above the city, was particularly beautiful. One of its most attractive features was an enormous body of water called Lake Conemaugh.

The lake had been formed by a man-made dam, constructed to supply water to a busy canal that ran between Johnstown and Pittsburgh. Made of stone and covered with tons of earth, the structure, the top of which was almost a thousand feet long, held more than twenty-five million tons of water.

Yet even though it was regarded as an engineering masterpiece, the dam had become unnecessary almost as soon as it was completed. In the early 1850s, travel by railroad was replacing travel by canal throughout America. When, in 1854, tracks were laid between Johnstown and Pittsburgh, the canal was abandoned.

For the next twenty-five years the dam remained basically unused. Then, in 1879, the five-hundred-acre lake, along with seventy acres that surrounded it, was purchased by some of the richest men in America, including steel magnate Andrew Carnegie and financiers Andrew Mellon and Henry Frick. Pleased with the beauty of the area and with the thought of fishing, boating, and swimming in the man-made lake, they decided to turn Lake Conemaugh into a private vacation retreat.

They named their resort the South Fork Fishing and Hunting Club, and by 1890 they had built a clubhouse that had 47 bedrooms, an enormous parlor, and a dining room that could seat up to 150 people. Sixteen of the sixty club members, seeking even greater comfort, had erected private "cottages" for themselves and their families. Some contained as many as seventeen rooms. All had huge porches that gave their owners magnificent views of the lake.

On several occasions members of the South Fork Club had been told that the dam was in a weakened condition as a result of years of inattention. As one Johnstown resident stated, "We were afraid of that lake. . . . No one could see the immense height to which that artificial dam had been built without fearing the tremendous power of the water behind it."

The men who owned the Cambria Iron Mills, the largest collection of steel mills in Johnstown, knew that if any section of the dam ever gave way, their factories and the rest of Johnstown would be in the direct path of whatever waters escaped. The president of the mills sent one of his engineers to inspect the dam and bring back a report.

The engineer's report revealed that a small break in the dam, caused by

Johnstown Flood Museum

Due to its low-lying location, Johnstown, Pennsylvania, had often experienced minor flooding. But no one in the community was prepared for what was to take place on May 30, 1889.

a heavy storm some thirty years earlier, had been inadequately repaired by stuffing branches, tree stumps, and sand into the hole. The report further stated that, should a period of unusually heavy rains occur and cause the lake to fill completely, that place in the dam would likely give way again. Additionally, the report showed that the valves controlling the height of the water in the lake were rusted and inoperative.

Alarmed by his engineer's findings, Cambria's president sent the report to the officers of the South Fork Club. They responded in a letter, stating simply ". . . you and your people are in no danger from our enterprise." It was a fatal miscalculation.

In May of 1889, the period of unusually heavy rains that Cambria's engineer had feared became a reality. By the last week of the month, eleven inches of rain had fallen in the area around Johnstown. On May 30 the skies opened yet again, and eight more inches of rain fell in that single day. By this time, Johnstown's streets had started to flood—but because they lived in a low-lying valley, the city's residents were used to minor flooding.

What the unsuspecting citizens of Johnstown did not know was that the eight inches of rain that had fallen on Memorial Day had filled the lake to capacity. The next day, as a group of spectators looked on, several cracks appeared in the dam. At 3:30 P.M. disaster struck. The entire dam collapsed at once with a roar that could be heard miles away. More than twenty-five million tons of water began a fourteen-mile journey down the mountain toward Johnstown, taking everything in its path along with it.

The first community struck by the forty-foot wall of water was the small town of East Conemaugh, which was the railroad center of the area. As the wave smashed into the town, twenty-three locomotives, each weighing about eighty tons, were tossed about like matchsticks. Houses in the town were immediately crushed. Many residents and more than twenty travelers sitting in the trains in the East Conemaugh railroad yards were killed.

Now carrying huge sections of houses and parts of trains along with it, the flood then slammed into the town of Woodvale. The town was the pride of the Cambria Iron Mills, built to house more than a thousand of the company's workers. Within minutes, all the houses were gone and some three hundred and fifty Woodvale citizens were dead. As newspaperman J. J. McLaurin would write, "Words cannot add impressiveness to the simple statement that only nine or ten families were not deprived of a father, mother, brother, or sister . . . two hundred and fifty habitations were swept away leaving *not one house* . . . Woodvale had ceased to be."

Then the flood roared into Johnstown. For the people of that town it was the beginning of a nightmare. "Scores, aye, hundreds of houses and parts of houses, wrecked and ruined structures . . . rushed down upon us," recalled one of Johnstown's ministers. "[It bore with it] barns, freight cars, city passenger cars, locomotive tenders, iron bridges, [factories], lumber, animals and human beings, dead and alive, and all kinds of wreckage, pitching, tossing, banging and smashing to pieces in one indiscriminate mass. We were in the midst of an angry, raging sea."

It took only ten minutes for the flood to unleash its fury on Johnstown.

"[The flood] came like a thief and was upon us before we were aware. Already when it reached us it had numbered its victims by the hundreds."
—*Johnstown Tribune*

Johnstown Flood Museum

A horrified Mrs. John Fenn saw her husband swept away as he tried to leave their house. Climbing to the roof with her seven children, she could only look on as a wave carried all of her children away to their deaths. Mrs. Fenn grabbed hold of a tar barrel that floated by and rode it until some heroic person swam to her and pulled her to safety.

Hundreds of Johnstown's citizens, many of them trapped in their houses, were carried along by the raging waters until they were slammed against a high stone railroad bridge that carried four tracks across the valley. One of the few structures strong enough to withstand the tons of water that smashed against it throughout the afternoon, the bridge became piled high with a thirty-foot mound of wrecked houses, telegraph poles, and other debris. Many people who had been swept along to the bridge climbed on top of the mound for safety. Then another disaster struck. At 6 P.M., the wreckage suddenly caught fire.

To this day, no one knows for certain what started the blaze. It was probably caused either by an overturned stove in one of the houses that had crashed against the bridge, or by oil from a ruptured railroad tank car that had piled into the debris. What *is* known is that hundreds of people died in the fire. "I saw . . . them," wrote one eyewitness, "as the flames approached, throw up their hands and fall backward into the fire, and those who had escaped drowning were reserved for the more horrible fate of being burned to death."

The day following the flood dawned bright and clear. The water in the streets was dropping rapidly. But the scene in Johnstown was one that its onlookers would never forget. "Everything about us was in . . . confusion," stated Reverend David J. Beale. "Here were uprooted trees, houses upturned or demolished, furniture of every description . . . bodies of horses, cattle and swine, corpses of men, women, and children, railroad carts and locomotives—overturned or on end, and pressing down upon the half-buried bodies of the drowned."

DEATH BY MOLASSES

On January 15, 1919, the section of Boston known as the North End was rocked by an ear-piercing, violent blast. A fifty-eight-foot high, ninety-foot wide storage tank containing 2.3 million gallons of molasses had suddenly exploded.

Waves of molasses, some fifteen feet high, flowed through the city streets, moving faster than people could run away. Within minutes, the river of syrup had crumbled the supports of an elevated railway, knocked over a fire station, and torn apart several freight cars.

Twenty-one people were killed and more than 150 suffered serious injuries. Some of the victims died when they were struck by huge fragments of metal thrown about by the explosion. Others drowned in the fast-moving tide of molasses. Horses trapped in the substance could not be freed and had to be shot.

It took months to remove the molasses from the streets. Thirty years later, residents claimed that, on a hot day, they could still smell molasses in their streets.

The city had been almost totally destroyed. More than twenty-two hundred people had been killed. One out of three bodies found were never identified. Almost a thousand were missing and never found. Ninety-nine families, ranging from two people to ten, were completely wiped out.

Very soon the indomitable spirit of the people of Johnstown became evident. The sounds of hammers, saws, and blasts of dynamite were heard as citizens began to rebuild their city. They were aided in their efforts by millions of dollars in money, food, and supplies that poured in from all parts of the world. Hundreds of people, some from many miles away, arrived to help in the relief and rebuilding efforts. Within six months, a new Johnstown had emerged.

"Everything in the line of the flood was displaced or swallowed up," said a Johnstown survivor. "Locomotives were tossed aside [and became] mere playthings for the whirlpool. Engines and cars were hidden beneath the timbers, brush and dirt."

Photographers who immediately rushed to Johnstown to record the aftermath of the disaster encountered some amazing sights.

The Johnstown flood remains one of America's most well-known disasters. Through dozens of books, songs, and movie and television reenactments, the story of what took place when the waters of Lake Conemaugh were let loose has remained etched in the national memory.

The same was not true of the South Fork Club. Newspapers around the nation wrote stories blaming the club for the disaster. The editor of the *Johnstown Tribune* echoed the thoughts of his fellow Johnstowners when he wrote, "We think we know what struck us and it was not the hand of [nature]. Our misfortune is the work of man. . . ." Faced with this barrage of bitter criticism, the South Fork Club closed down. In 1891 the land belonging to the club was divided and sold at auction.

Drought and its accompanying dust storms have long plagued
people throughout the world. The prolonged drought that took place
in the 1930s was the most severe ever to hit the United States.

THREE

DROUGHTS AND DUST
Disaster from the Parched Earth

Too much rain leads to catastrophes like the Johnstown flood. Too little rain creates another kind of disaster. When rainfall is nonexistent or far below normal, crops wither in the fields and livestock die from thirst.

The Great Plains area of the United States has a long history of periods without adequate rainfall. The pioneers who settled that region in the last half of the 1800s discovered that droughts and their accompanying dust storms were perhaps the greatest challenges in building new lives in the American West. None of these settlers, however, experienced so great a drought-caused disaster as did those Americans who lived on the southern plains in the 1930s.

THE DUST BOWL

From the 1840s through the 1880s, millions of people, seeking to escape the overcrowding and poor working conditions of the eastern cities, headed west. They were spurred on by the United States government, which gave 160 acres of free land to anyone who would turn his new property into a working farm.

Once on their new land, these pioneers encountered incredible hardships: searing heat in summer, raging blizzards in winter, swarms of locusts, and winds that never seemed to stop. But the territory to which they had come contained some of the richest soil in the world.

In many ways, these pioneer farmers and the generations that followed them succeeded too well. Year after year they planted crop after crop. With each crop a little more soil was stripped from the ground. Early in the 1930s the farmers began to pay the price for their years of overfarming and neglect of the soil.

In 1931 the vast American prairie was hit by an enormous drought. Almost no rain fell, and crops died as the dry soil cracked in the sun. Temperatures rose to 100°F for weeks at a time. Hardest hit of all were the farm families who lived in the southern plain states of Colorado, New Mexico, Kansas, Texas, and Oklahoma.

By 1933, the continuing lack of rain had turned much of the topsoil, already weakened by decades of overfarming, into dust. The ever-present prairie winds picked up the dust and lifted it into the air, creating that type of environmental disaster appropriately called a dust storm. For three years, one after another of these storms struck the area, turning the 97-million-acre region into a gigantic dust bowl.

The dust storms were terrifying to behold. As one historian described it, "The skies were darkened. . . . The dry soil drifted like snow; automobiles

The dust storms began on the Great Plains, but strong winds carried the dust as far away as Washington, D.C.

had to use their headlights at noon; families stuffed door and window cracks to keep from being choked. . . ." A Kansas woman recalled, "All we could do was just sit in our dusty chairs, gaze at each other through the fog that filled the room and watch that fog settle slowly and silently, covering everything—including ourselves."

Carried along by howling winds, the dust settled on areas as far away as Baltimore, Maryland, and Washington, D.C. Ships far out in the Atlantic were covered with the powder.

To those who lived in the states of the southern plains, the drought and the dust storms were nothing short of a calamity. While few people in the area actually died during the storms, many became ill from inhaling the dust. The Red Cross was forced to open field hospitals to care for those who had come down with what was termed "dust pneumonia." In order to protect their mouths and noses, people throughout the region began wearing masks.

Library of Congress

Library of Congress

As 97 million acres of once-rich farmland turned to dust, millions of people were forced to leave their farms, take to the road, and look for work in the Far West.

Farmers suffered the most. As the drought continued, the streams and ponds on their farms dried up and their pastures withered away, leaving their cattle, hogs, and other livestock without sufficient water or food. Worst of all, the once-rich soil upon which they had planted their crops was rapidly disappearing. In 1935, at the height of the drought and dust storms, 850 million tons of topsoil were carried away by the winds.

With no crops to sell, the owners could not continue to make payments to the banks that had loaned them the money for their land, their homes, their livestock, and their equipment.

With their land destroyed and their property taken over by the banks, millions had no choice but to leave the farms that their families had worked for generations. Some five hundred thousand headed for California, hoping to find jobs picking apples and other fruit in that state's many orchards. These farmers had come to the southern plains and carved out new lives in what had once been a wilderness. Now, as they left, their abandoned farms stood as monuments both to the way the land had been misused and to the forces of nature.

Because many had come from Oklahoma, the hardest hit of all the states, the newspapers labeled the migrants Okies. Most found that conditions in California were no better than the places they had left behind. Those who managed to find work in the orchards were forced to toil long hours at backbreaking tasks for very little pay. Workers suffered through long stretches without any work at all. Once proud owners of their own prosperous farms, they were treated with scorn by California fruit pickers who saw them as a threat to their own jobs.

The United States government, having learned many lessons from the plains disaster, was taking steps toward preventing such catastrophes in the future. Huge irrigation projects were being launched, eventually bringing millions of gallons of water to the drought-stricken lands. The United States Forest Service was beginning a program of planting more than 200 million

A PHOTOGRAPHIC RECORD

Sometimes, unexpected developments arise of out a national disaster. In response to the Great Depression of the 1930s, the U.S. government created the Farm Security Administration (FSA), whose goal it was to aid the millions of farmers caught up in hard times. One of the divisions of the FSA was the Historical Section, given the task of taking photographs of relief workers helping the farmers. The head of the Historical Section, a man named Roy Stryker, hired some of the nation's most talented photographers to take the pictures. Included among these people were such future giants of photography as Dorothea Lange, Walker Evans, Arthur Rothstein, Russell Lee, and Marion Post Wolcott.

Realizing that his photographic corps represented one of the greatest arrays of photographic talent ever assembled, Stryker decided to go well beyond simply having them take pictures of relief workers in action. "Your goal," he told them, "is to introduce America to Americans." Their pictures of the hardships brought on by the economic disaster, particularly in the Dust Bowl areas, shocked the nation and inspired Congress to increase its efforts to help the people in this region.

But tens of thousands of their photographs also provided a striking visual portrait of all aspects of American life. Perhaps most important, hundreds of the images dramatically revealed the indomitable spirit of the American people, even in the face of the most difficult circumstances. As Stryker stated after viewing most of the pictures, "Despair versus dignity; I believe that dignity wins out."

Housed today in the Library of Congress, the FSA collection, containing more than 270,000 images, remains arguably the greatest single collection of photographs ever compiled.

Photographer Dorothea Lange took this picture of a mother and her children who had lost their home due to drought. Lange's ability to capture the look of uncertainty on the woman's face made the image particularly powerful. Widely published in newspapers and magazines, the photograph became a poignant symbol of the Great Depression.

Sandler Collection

Like other major American disasters, the Dust Bowl experience became the subject of numerous books, songs, plays, and motion pictures. The most famous of all these depictions is John Steinbeck's Pulitzer Prize–winning novel, *The Grapes of Wrath*.

trees in the dried-out areas. The trees would serve as windbreaks and would also help keep the topsoil from blowing away in the wind.

Most important, the government began educating those farmers who had remained in the region about more responsible methods of farming. Agricultural experts introduced farmers to the practice of planting certain types of crops that actually put nutrients back into the earth, preserving the precious topsoil. These experts also demonstrated new techniques of plowing the land in a way that discouraged erosion and helped the soil retain moisture. The government also encouraged farmers to adopt the practice of planting only half their acreage in any one year while keeping the other half covered with rich grass that enriched the land.

Ironically, while it had been nature in the form of drought and dust storms that had caused so great a disaster, it was also nature that supplied the final step in the recovery of the devastated lands. In 1941, after almost ten years of drought, it began raining. Over several months, water from a long series of steady downpours soaked deep into the earth. The parched prairie land turned green again.

Tens of thousands who had fled to California gradually began to make their way home. Most no longer owned their land. But with the same kind of spirit that their pioneer ancestors had shown, they worked, saved their money, and in many cases were able once again to purchase their own farms. This time they were armed with the knowledge to maintain the land wisely. After one of the most traumatic decades in the nation's history, the agony of the Dust Bowl was finally over.

Fire has always presented the greatest danger to American woodlands. In the year 2000 alone, more than 8 million acres of American forests were destroyed by fire.

FIRE
The Ever-Present Danger

Fire has sustained and benefited human beings from the days of the cave dwellers. But fire has also been the cause of many of this country's greatest catastrophes. Among the most tragic have been:

• The 1911 Triangle Shirtwaist Factory fire in New York City. One hundred and forty-six immigrant women garment workers died. The overcrowded building provided no means of escape.

• The 1903 Iroquois Theatre fire in Chicago. More than six hundred people, mostly children, were killed in a theater built by architects more interested in the beauty of the structure than its patrons' safety.

• The 1942 Coconut Grove nightclub fire in Boston. About five hundred patrons lost their lives because the club's owners had locked many of the exits to prevent people from sneaking into the establishment without paying.

• The 1944 Hartford, Connecticut, circus fire. One hundred and sixty-eight men, women, and children perished because the circus's owners had failed to fireproof the giant tent in which the circus was being held.

The most infamous of all American fires, however, is known as the Great Chicago Fire of 1871. It was a disaster that took the lives of some three hundred people and totally destroyed about three and a half square miles in the heart of one of the nation's greatest cities. What is far less known, however, is that on the very same night that sections of Chicago burned down, a much more serious and disastrous fire took place in the forests of Wisconsin.

THE WISCONSIN FOREST FIRE

The words on a tablet in a cemetery in Peshtigo, Wisconsin, tell the sad story of a devastating catastrophe.

"On the night of October 8, 1871," the tablet reads, "Peshtigo, a booming town of 1700 people, was wiped out of existence in the greatest forest fire disaster in American history. . . . Every building in the community was lost. The tornado of fire claimed at least 800 lives in the area [alone]. Many of the victims lie here. The memory of 350 unidentified men, women, and children is preserved in a nearby mass grave."

Until the night that disaster struck, Peshtigo had been a thriving lumber town. Located on both sides of the Peshtigo River, it was surrounded for miles by some of the richest forests of pine and spruce trees in America.

Before the Peshtigo fire, hundreds of lumberjacks worked in the miles of forest surrounding the town. The lumber they produced was used to build homes and businesses throughout America.

In those areas where there were openings in the woods, settlers had established well-kept farms.

The main business in Peshtigo was the sawmill and the factory complex owned by the Peshtigo Company. Every week, the firm's sawmills shipped lumber to cities and towns throughout the country. At the same time, its factory produced more household items than any other woodenwares company in the nation. And things were getting even better.

In the early fall of 1871, the Chicago and Northern Railroad began extending its tracks through Peshtigo to places in Wisconsin and Michigan located on the Great Lakes. As lumbermen cleared the thick woods that lay in the path of the advancing railroad, they produced enormous mounds of tree limbs and pine needles. They then set fire to the mounds and moved to the next area to be cleared, leaving the wood to burn down eventually to ash. Before long, there were scores of large, unattended fires burning in the forest.

Library of Congress

In the late 1800s, it was common practice for lumbermen to create piles of debris, which they would then set ablaze before moving on to new parts of the forest. As the people of Peshtigo sadly discovered, it was a most dangerous practice.

Strange as it might seem, leaving piles of burning debris unattended in the woods was not unusual. The lumbermen did so regularly in the normal course of their work, relying on the region's above-average snowfall and rainstorms to keep the blazes under control. But during the winter of 1871 there had been almost no snow. The summer that followed was just as dry. As October approached, the forest was turning into a tinderbox.

With no rain to keep them in check, some of the fires from the burning debris were beginning to spread underground, attacking and gnawing away at the roots of the tall trees. In the swampy areas of the forest, the unde- tected fires were burning from one to three feet beneath the earth.

By October 5, the air for miles around Peshtigo was filled with dense smoke. The afternoon sky glowed red and ashes began drifting down into the town. Thousands of birds, driven from their roosts in the trees, flew madly about. On October 7, as the people of Peshtigo prayed for rain, the editor of the town's newspaper reported, "Fires are still lurking in the woods . . . ready to pounce upon any portion of the village in the event of an unfavorable wind. . . . Unless we have rain soon, God only knows how soon a conflagration may sweep this town." He did not have to wait long for his answer.

The very next night, the woods southwest of Peshtigo burst into flame. What was now one gigantic fire sped toward the town. The people living on the farms in the clearings were the first victims. As they looked into the sky they witnessed a sight that no one in the region had ever seen. An enor- mous round, dark mass of air was whirling about. It swirled over their heads and then exploded with a gigantic roar. Pillars of flame shot high above the treetops and then dropped down upon the people below. Almost everyone on these farms was instantly killed.

Within minutes the fire was upon Peshtigo. "[There] came a low rum- bling noise like the distant approach of a train of cars," reported the *Marinette-Peshtigo Eagle*. "The noise increased to a heavy roar . . . like the noise of thunder or a mighty wind and the startled people ran into the streets to ascertain the cause. The long dread of fire, that [had been present for days], at once suggested to most minds what the danger really was. Mothers hastily snatched their children from their beds and partially dressed them. Some had long had their valuables packed in trunks in anticipation of fire, and others began to pack up their goods. The men mustered in squads and prepared to fight the fire. . . ."

But it was too late. The fire was beginning to race through Peshtigo. What's more, it was accompanied by the same strange phenomenon witnessed by the farmers outside of town. "When I heard the roar of the approaching tornado [of fire]," recalled townsman Alfred Griffin, "I ran out of my house and saw a black balloon-shaped object. . . . When it reached my

In their rush to find safety in the Peshtigo River, many people were trampled to death.

FIRESTORM

Most forests contain marshes and swamps that harbor natural gases. As a fire moves along these areas it picks up the highly flammable gases. Because the fire uses up most of the oxygen near the ground, the gases do not immediately burn. But when the pockets of gas are carried high into the air by the heat of the fire, they encounter large amounts of oxygen and explode violently.

Those who fight forest fires today call these explosions "blowups." They are more commonly known as firestorms. It was this deadly phenomenon that so terrified people in and around Peshtigo and that rained so much death and destruction upon them that fateful day in 1871.

house it seemed to explode, with a loud noise, belching out fire on every side, and in an instant my house was on fire in every part."

Immediately, cries of "To the river! To the river!" were heard everywhere. It seemed to be the only chance of surviving the inferno. Hundreds plunged into the Peshtigo River's frigid waters. It was indeed the best place to be. But it was still far from safe. As the wind blew huge sheets of flame across the water, scores of people were burned to death. Others, caught in the crush of people, were knocked beneath the water and drowned. Still others were killed by heavy debris, carried along by the wind.

Rather than seeking safety in the river, hundreds of other residents from both sides of the town had rushed to the bridge that spanned the waters. As they raced to the middle of the bridge, they and the horses, cows, dogs, and wild animals that had followed them collided head-on. Then the bridge caught fire. Scores were trampled as they tried to avoid the flames. Others were killed when they jumped from the bridge and drowned in the river.

It took only three hours for the worst forest fire in American history to destroy the once-thriving town of Peshtigo.

The disaster at the bridge was made complete when the burning structure collapsed, crushing all those beneath it.

Things were no better for those who had sought shelter elsewhere. Some fifty people had crowded into the town's only brick building. As the temperature from the inferno that surrounded them reached an incredible 2,000° F, they were all literally baked alive.

Many desperate fathers, aware that they had been too late in getting their families to the water, lowered their wives and children into the wells beside their homes. But the relentless flames, seeking any opening, found their way into every one of the wells, killing all inside them.

It had taken only three hours for the most disastrous forest fire in American history to wipe Peshtigo out of existence. As survivor George Watson stated, "Not a hen-coop or a dry-goods box was left." Perhaps the most telling description of the catastrophe was that provided by one of the region's newspapers a week after the tragedy. "Yesterday morning . . . ," reported the paper, "we visited the once beautiful and thriving little village of Peshtigo. It contained about [seventeen hundred] people, and was one of the busiest, liveliest and one of the most enterprising communities along the Bay shore. Standing amid the charred and blackened embers, with the frightfully mutilated corpses of men, women, children, oxen, cows, dogs, swine and fowls; every house, shed, barn, out-house or structure of any kind swept from the earth . . . ; our emotions cannot be described in any language."

The night after the fire, in a terrible twist of fate, the rain that the people of Peshtigo had so frantically prayed for finally began to fall. It was the start of the longest and heaviest period of rainfall Wisconsin had ever experienced. But it had come twenty-four hours too late. The town was gone. As many as fifteen hundred people in the area had been killed, eight hundred in Peshtigo and its surrounding woods alone. It was the greatest loss of life in any forest fire in United States history.

Hurricane Andrew was one of the most costly storms ever to strike the United States.
It destroyed some 80,000 homes and severely damaged more than 55,000 others.

HURRICANES
Nature's Fury Unleashed

The dictionary defines a hurricane as "a severe tropical cyclone with winds exceeding seventy-five miles per hour, originating in the tropical regions of the Atlantic Ocean or Caribbean Sea, traveling north, northwest, or northeast . . . and usually involving heavy rains." The most severe hurricanes are those that are accompanied by what is known as a storm surge. These surges bring with them enormous waves and abnormally high tides. As they destroy homes and buildings along the coastline and then sweep inland, storm surges cause even more destruction than the hurricane-force winds.

Certain areas of the United States, particularly Florida, Texas, the Carolinas, and the coastal states of New England, have always been prone to hurricanes. In September 1928, for example, after devastating several Caribbean islands and the Bahamas, a hurricane made landfall in Palm

Beach, Florida, destroying some eight thousand homes and killing more than twenty-four hundred people. In September 1938, a hurricane that struck without any warning smashed into the New England coast and Long Island, New York. Although it lasted only a few hours, the storm destroyed more than forty-five hundred homes and killed at least seven hundred people.

In recent decades, hurricanes have been given human names. The most devastating of these more modern disasters was Hurricane Andrew, which in August 1992 cut a swath through sixty miles of southern Florida. By 1992, weather-predicting methods and equipment had been vastly improved and fewer than fifty people were killed. Still, Andrew destroyed an area larger than the city of Chicago and caused $125 billion in damage.

Staggering as these figures are, they pale in comparison to the toll taken by the most disastrous hurricane ever to strike the United States. It took place long before such storms were given names. But it will never be forgotten.

THE GALVESTON HURRICANE

Up until the year 1900, Galveston, Texas, located on an island in the Gulf of Mexico and connected to the mainland by a two-mile causeway, had been known for three things. The notorious French pirate Jean LaFitte had founded it in 1817. It featured world-class beaches. And it was rapidly becoming one of America's leading ports. On Saturday, September 8, 1900, Galveston would add a fourth claim to fame. It would become the site of the nation's most devastating hurricane.

The storm began innocently enough, starting out as what the United States Weather Bureau described as a "tropical disturbance over Cuba" that

FACTS ABOUT THE GALVESTON HURRICANE

- Some fifteen hundred acres of the Galveston shoreline—containing homes, restaurants, stores, and the city's famed beach facilities—were swept clean by the storm.

- More than 3,630 houses in Galveston were completely destroyed.

- More people were killed in the hurricane than in the Johnstown flood, the San Francisco earthquake, and the Chicago fire *combined*.

- The seawall built to protect Galveston from future hurricanes was completed in 1910. It stood seventeen feet above the beach. In front of it was a barrier twenty-seven feet high, made of granite boulders.

- In completing the monumental task of literally raising more than twenty-one hundred Galveston buildings to prevent a repeat of the 1900 disaster's toll, workers used eleven million pounds of fill.

was headed for Florida. Even when the national weather bureau changed its forecast and predicted that the storm would likely strike Galveston after hitting Florida, most people in the city remained unconcerned. Their thirty-mile island had often been flooded by storms. When that happened, many people in the city would simply go off on vacation.

What the people of Galveston didn't know was that the tropical depression had suddenly developed into a full-blown hurricane. It had also changed direction, taking it west across open Gulf waters, and was packing winds in excess of 135 miles per hour.

At 4 A.M. on Saturday, September 8, Joseph Cline, one of two brothers working in the Galveston weather office, suddenly awoke with what he later described as a "sense of impending disaster" and looked out his window. He was shocked by what he saw. Waters from the Gulf were splashing across the backyard. Since the time he had gone to bed the tide had risen more than five feet above normal. Joseph immediately woke his brother Isaac, and while Joseph raced off to man the weather station, Isaac hitched his horse to a cart and hurried off to warn residents who lived along the shore to leave their homes. Not only did most of those with whom he spoke ignore his warnings, but hundreds of Galveston citizens actually went down to the beach to watch the storm come ashore.

Shortly after 9 A.M. it began to rain lightly. But by noon, the winds had grown to gale force and it was raining harder than most longtime Galvestonians had ever seen. By 5:30 P.M., winds were blowing at up to 130 miles per hour, houses were being torn apart, and parts of buildings and trees were blowing through the air. Galveston was in the beginning stages of the fiercest hurricane it or any other American city had ever experienced.

Soon things got even worse. At 6:30 P.M., a storm surge in advance of the full brunt of the hurricane sent more than four feet of water crashing down on the island. Most of those who had remained in their homes along the shore and those who had lingered on the beach were washed away. In the city itself scores of houses that had withstood the storm thus far were ripped from their foundations, taking the lives of all those inside them.

As the storm grew in intensity, more people were killed. Hundreds had sought refuge in the city's churches, but as the unprecedented winds continued without letup, almost all these buildings, most of them made of wood, collapsed and crushed those who had sought shelter in them. Ninety children and ten nuns lost their lives when the city's largest orphanage was blown down upon them. Even the hospitals were not safe. More than a hundred patients in one hospital died when the killer winds tore through the building.

In many sections of the city, the hurricane acted as if it was on a

"There is almost nothing standing south of Avenue N. Everything is gone."
—*R. Wilbur Goodman, Galveston resident*

"It's a sight I hope I shall never see again. Destruction and desolation; wreckage strewn everywhere . . . I had to search those ruins for all I had held dear."
—*Arnold R. Wolfram, Galveston resident*

Almost immediately after the disaster, both the army and the Red Cross set up tents to temporarily house those who had lost just about everything.

planned path of destruction, making its way from street to street. While most of the large homes in these sections were simply crushed to bits, the smaller ones were picked up by the winds and blown into the air, often landing in the next street. All this took place while the streets lay under some fourteen feet of water from the still-surging tide. For people living in these areas, there was little chance of survival.

As one family looked out a window in their home, which fortunately was still standing, they saw a man go by on horseback in the middle of the street. Only the horse's head was out of the water. Scores of people were seen running through the streets completely naked. They had somehow made it through a wind so strong that it had torn off all their clothes.

One woman was carried out into the Gulf in her wooden bathtub. Thought to be yet another casualty of the storm, she was brought safely back to shore on the next morning's tide. Another woman was also given up for lost when the roof blew off her house and she couldn't be found. Miraculously, the roofless attic of the house had remained intact and the woman had protected herself through the night by crouching underneath the attic's timbers. All this time she had her pet parrot on her shoulder. In the morning, rescuers were led to her by the parrot's repeated cries of "Polly, pretty Polly."

Perhaps the most amazing survival story of all was that of a Mrs. Henry Heideman. Eight months pregnant, she was in her house when it collapsed in the wind, apparently killing her three-year-old son and her husband. Mrs. Heideman dug herself out of the wreckage and made her way onto a roof that was floating by. But the roof soon collided with another floating object that turned out to be a large trunk. Miraculously, Mrs. Heideman slid off the roof and right down into the trunk, which proceeded to carry her along the water until it banged into an upper window of a convent. The nuns inside the convent dragged Mrs. Heideman inside, wrapped her in warm clothing, and put her to bed. Then she went into labor.

At the same time, a man who had sought refuge in a tree in the convent courtyard heard a child crying in the waters beneath the tree and hauled him out to safety. Within a moment he recognized the youngster. It was his own nephew, Mrs. Heideman's three-year-old son. Mrs. Heideman's baby was safely delivered. She had her three-year-old son back. But her husband was never found.

The day after the hurricane those Galvestonians who had been fortunate enough to get any sleep at all awoke to a bright sky and a calm Gulf. But in some areas of the city not a single building was left standing. One resident described it this way: "On Sunday morning after the storm was all over," he said, "I went out into the streets and saw the most horrible sights that you

One of the most gruesome tasks was the removal of bodies from the wreckage. It was an ordeal that went on for months.

can ever imagine. I gazed upon dead bodies lying here and there. The houses all blown into pieces; women, men, and children all walking the streets in weak condition with bleeding heads and bodies and feet all torn to pieces with glass where they had been treading through the debris of fallen buildings. And when I got to the Gulf and bay coast I saw *hundreds* of houses all destroyed with dead bodies lying in the ruins, little babies in their mothers' arms."

Those who wandered down to the shore were shocked to find that huge areas of the beach had been washed away. The long causeway connecting Galveston with the Texas mainland had vanished. In one section of the remaining beach more than a thousand bodies were being placed on a huge funeral pyre so that they could be cremated to prevent disease from spreading throughout the city. Other bodies were being loaded onto tugboats that would take them far out into the Gulf to be given a burial at sea. The death toll from the hurricane was almost beyond belief. Out of some thirty-eight thousand Galveston residents, more than six thousand had been killed. Between four thousand and six thousand people living along other areas of the Texas coastline had also lost their lives.

Many people did their best to help. When news of what had happened in Galveston reached the outside world, millions of dollars in aid were donated to the city and its victims. Volunteers spent months helping Galvestonians clean up and begin to rebuild their city.

The Galveston storm was the worst hurricane ever to strike the United States. But out of it came lessons important not only to Galveston but to the rest of the nation. Within a few years, Galveston erected a three-mile-long seawall along its coastline, built to protect the city from flooding in even the most severe storms. Soon, other coastal cities in the United States would follow suit. Perhaps the greatest example of the spirit of Galveston's people took place shortly after the seawall was completed. Determined to protect future Galvestonians from suffering as they had from living in so low-lying an area, they took on a herculean task. They successfully jacked up more than twenty-one hundred buildings, one of which weighed three thousand tons, and placed millions of cubic yards of sand beneath them. The people of Galveston had not only raised their spirits; they had literally raised their city as well.

Blizzards can bring even the largest cities to a standstill. This was the scene in
New York City immediately after the great snowstorm of 1888 finally ended.

SIX.

BLIZZARDS
Disasters from the Sky

Skiers look forward to snow-filled winters. Children have always loved sledding, sleigh rides, and snowmen or snowball fights. But excessive amounts of snow, particularly that which comes down in fierce storms called blizzards, can cause real problems. They result in the loss of electricity and other power, force schools and businesses to close, and, particularly in cities, bring transportation to a halt. At their worst, blizzards cause extensive damage and loss of life.

Weather experts define a blizzard as "a violent windstorm accompanied by intense cold and driving snow." In 1888 America's largest city was hit with one of the most terrifying blizzards of all time.

THE BLIZZARD OF '88

Saturday, March 10, 1888, was a beautiful day in New York, with temperatures rising above 60° F. It was, in fact, the warmest day in what was turning out to be the mildest winter in more than seventeen years.

From deep in the Gulf of Mexico, however, an enormous amount of warm moisture was making its way northward up the East Coast. At the very same time, another huge mass of freezing cold air was moving toward New York southward from Canada. The cold air was traveling at the unusually high speed of eighty miles per hour. The result of two such masses of air colliding is a ferocious blizzard. These weather events, fairly common in the Great Plains states such as Kansas, Nebraska, and North and South Dakota, are rare on the East Coast. And the weather forecasters of 1888, working with equipment far more primitive that what is available today, were totally unaware of the oncoming disaster.

On Sunday, March 11, the United States Weather Bureau issued a forecast for New York calling for light snow. Monday, the forecast further stated, would be "generally fair and colder, preceded by partial cloudiness near the coast." Rather than snowing, it actually rained heavily almost all day Sunday. But during the evening, temperatures plummeted, the winds began to howl, and by midnight the rains had turned to heavy snow.

When New Yorkers awoke on the following morning they were greeted by an astonishing sight. Just two days after unseasonably warm temperatures, their outside thermometers read well below zero. A raging blizzard was underway, and the city was rapidly being buried in drifts driven by hurricane-force winds.

Tens of thousand of people still set out for work. Perhaps this was because they were New Yorkers, used to dealing with all the challenges of living in the world's most modern city. Most New Yorkers had come to believe that almost nothing was impossible. How could a mere blizzard keep them from carrying out their work?

They were dead wrong. By noon the city was covered with three and a half feet of snow, which showed no signs of letting up. Most offices and stores were forced to shut down. Telephone and telegraph poles snapped like twigs, taking their electrical wires down with them and shutting off all communications. The horse-drawn trolleys could not make their way through the snow-filled streets. The ferries could not take passengers across New York Harbor to outlying suburbs. Even the Brooklyn Bridge had to be closed. The tens of thousands who had confidently set off to work that morning found themselves stranded, desperate to find a way home.

Many people, including twenty mailmen determined to carry out their duties, fainted and had to be rescued by New York City policemen so they wouldn't freeze to death. Throughout the storm, the policemen performed heroically. But there was only so much they could do. Scores of men and women, forced to fight their way through the cold and the enormous drifts of snow, suffered heart attacks and died. Others were electrocuted when they stepped on fallen electrical wires that were buried beneath the snow. Still others were killed when they were struck by tree branches, signs, and other heavy objects propelled through the air by the unrelenting winds.

More than one person, struggling to find some kind of shelter, tripped over something and then discovered that "something" to be the frozen body of a fellow New Yorker. Others, blinded by the driving snow, found themselves walking in circles, close to collapse, before being rescued or stumbling upon a place where they could get out of the storm.

A man named C. H. MacDonald fell into a large snowdrift. Since the drift was quite soft, MacDonald was amazed to find that when he made his way out, he had a large gash in his head. Digging into the drift he discovered that his head had struck the sharp hoof of an unfortunate horse that had been killed and buried by the snow. After the blizzard was over,

MacDonald amused his friends by bragging that he was the only person in New York ever to be kicked in the head by a dead horse.

Another man, attempting to make his way home on foot, was overcome by the blizzard and bumped into a lamppost, where he passed out. His face began to freeze to the post but, luckily, he awoke in time to free himself and stagger to his house. When he awoke the next morning he discovered that his false teeth were missing. When the storm was finally over, he returned to the spot where he had almost died and found his teeth still frozen to the lamppost.

Most of the incidents that emerged from the blizzard, however, were far from humorous. At the time of the storm, U. S. senator Roscoe Conkling, a founder of the Republican Party, was one of the most famous men in America. At the height of the blizzard, Conkling tried to walk from his New York office to his club, where he felt he could wait out the storm in comfort. The club was only a few blocks away, but when the senator attempted to cross a park he became trapped in a giant snowdrift. "For nearly twenty minutes I was stuck there," Conkling told a reporter later that evening. "I came as near giving up and sinking down there to die as a man can and

New York firemen worked valiantly to reach those in danger. But their efforts were often thwarted by the raging blizzard.

Harper's

RECORD SNOWFALLS

- Silver Lake, Colorado, holds the distinction of being the community in the United States to record the largest single snowfall in a single day. On April 24, 1921, Silver Lake received a whopping seventy-six inches of snow—more than six feet.

- The greatest one-year snowfall in one locale in the United States occurred from February 1971 to February 1972 in Mt. Rainier National Park in Washington State. During that period, 1,122 inches of snow fell in the park.

- The longest-lasting blizzard in American history took place in the western United States in 1949. The storm lasted a record seven weeks, with blizzard conditions continuing from January 2 to February 19.

- In 1947 a fierce storm buried New York City in 25.8 inches of snow. According to the weather bureau, that was 4.9 inches more than the city received in the blizzard of '88. But then the weather bureau made an interesting announcement. They stated that since so little wind accompanied the 1947 storm, it could not officially be classified as a blizzard.

not do it. Somehow I got out and made my way along. When I reached the New York Club, I was covered all over with ice and packed snow. . . . It took me three hours to make the journey." It was a story that seemed to have a happy ending. But the next day Conkling became ill from having overexerted himself and died shortly afterward.

People who boarded trains at one of the four elevated railway lines were far from safe. One by one, the trains on all four of the els (as they were called) were forced to a halt by the snow, stranding more than fifteen thousand people high above the streets of New York. Here the good and the bad of human nature came into play. Aware that the stranded passengers faced

The historic snowstorm blanketed the entire Northeast. This young student at a private school in Connecticut posed beside a snow tunnel that she and her classmates constructed.

the real possibility of freezing to death, many young men risked their own lives by hoisting ladders up to the cars. They climbed the ladders in the blinding snow and carried countless passengers to safety. But others, seeing in the disaster a way to line their pockets, hoisted ladders, climbed up to the trapped victims, and then refused to take everyone down unless each person they rescued paid them a twenty-dollar fee.

Train passengers bound to New York from Buffalo aboard the *Flyer* had a terrible experience. When the *Flyer*'s engineer spotted enormous mounds of snow ahead of him on the tracks he decided that, if he opened the throttle to full speed, he could force his way through. He was wrong. As the train came to a jarring halt, hot coals poured out of a woodstove in one of the cars, setting it on fire. Panicked passengers immediately raced out of the car into the raging blizzard. Blinded by the snow, they headed for the safety of nearby houses, but some lost their way and froze to death. Their bodies were not found until the drifts finally began to melt.

The Blizzard of '88 was so enormous that it was months before the last snow disappeared from the ground. Frozen bodies were still being discovered in the heart of New York City in June. In some places outside the city, snow had piled as high as thirty feet and there were still three-foot drifts as late as mid-July.

When authorities were finally able to assess the toll taken by the "white hurricane," as the storm was also called, their findings revealed that what had been forecast as a "slight snowstorm" had turned out to be one of the greatest disasters in the history of the nation's largest city. More than two hundred ships and boats had been sunk in New York Harbor and other waterways. Thousands of livestock, birds, and other animals had been killed. Property damage was in the tens of millions. And more than four hundred people had lost their lives.

There were, however, some positive outcomes of the disaster. In the twenty-five years following the blizzard, New York moved its telephone, telegraph, and power lines underground. The city also constructed the largest subway system in America. Future storms could not be prevented. But never again, even in the worst weather, would New Yorkers be unable to communicate with each other or travel safely within their city.

In an age before television and radio, people relied on newspapers to keep them informed. New York papers issued special editions detailing the mammoth storm that had struck the city.

As in almost all previous disasters, hundreds of people risked their own health and safety by tending to those who had been struck down by the 1918 influenza epidemic.

DISEASE
Nature's Greatest Disaster

If one were to ask a group of people which type of natural disaster has, throughout history, killed more people than any other, their answers probably would include earthquakes or volcanoes or hurricanes or floods. Yet the truth is that infectious disease has devastated more human populations than any other natural disaster.

In the Middle Ages, a plague known as the Black Death wiped out almost one-third of all the people in Europe and Asia. In the period following the European colonization of Central America, a staggering 90 percent of the native population died of infectious diseases.

Disease has conquered armies as well as civilizations. When Napoleon Bonaparte invaded Russia in 1812, he sent five hundred thousand troops on a long march to conquer Moscow. Some three hundred and eighty thousand of these soldiers were killed, not from enemy bullets but from outbreaks of both typhus and dysentery—the result of their drinking dirty water.

Among the most common forms of infectious disease is that known as influenza—or, more commonly, the flu. Influenza is a word that comes from the Italian phrase *influenza di freddo*, meaning "influence of the cold." Until the early twentieth century, the flu was commonly regarded as more of a nuisance than a deadly disease. Relatively few people had ever died from it. But in 1918, that all changed. In that year, the world experienced the outbreak of an unknown strain of the illness. Before the epidemic ran its course, at least 23 million people lost their lives.

THE INFLUENZA EPIDEMIC OF 1918–19

No one knows exactly where the influenza epidemic of 1918–19 began. What is certain is that soldiers fighting in Europe in World War I, including American troops, began to fall victim to the flu in the autumn of 1918. This type of influenza was so contagious that entire military units came down with it and many soldiers died. As soldiers were sent home with the flu they brought the sickness with them, spreading it around the world. Within a few months, more people had died from this mysterious form of influenza than had been killed in all four years of bitter fighting in Europe.

The first outbreaks of the disease in the United States began on military bases. In the last two months of 1918, 40 percent of the navy came down with the deadly illness. More than 35 percent of all the men in the army caught the disease.

Military officials looked on helplessly as the flu took its toll. One army officer stationed at Fort Devens, Massachusetts, described "hundreds of

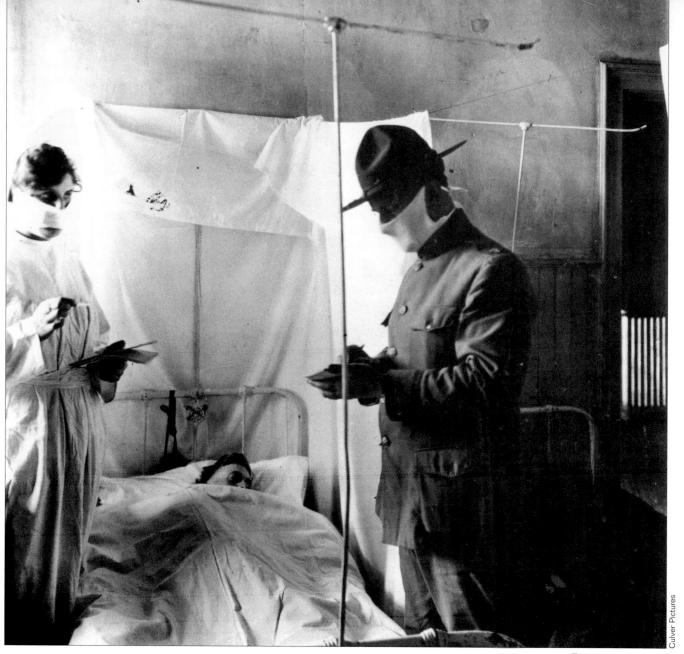

The disastrous flu epidemic of 1918–19 probably got its start among soldiers fighting in World War I.

stalwart young men in the uniform of their country coming into the wards of the hospital in groups of ten or more. They are placed on cots until every bed is full, yet others crowd in. Their faces soon wear a bluish cast; a distressing cough brings up the blood. . . . In the morning the dead bodies are stacked about the morgue like cord wood."

Matters got even worse as the epidemic spread from the army camps and naval bases to cities and towns throughout the nation. In the last week of

BATTLING DISEASE

The flu disaster of 1918—19 inspired scientists and medical researchers around the world to find new ways of identifying and stopping the spread of infectious disease. In the last fifty years, one of the most effective organizations in this battle has been a United States government agency called the Centers for Disease Control and Prevention (CDC). Founded during World War II, one of its early accomplishments was the establishment of a laboratory to prevent what happened in 1918—19 by diagnosing certain types of diseases that returning servicemen might bring home from overseas.

Driven by its mission "to improve the quality of life for all Americans," the CDC wages all-out war against infectious disease by employing scientists and many others. It puts all of these people through an intense training program and prepares many of them to respond immediately to outbreaks of disease no matter where in the world they occur.

Among its many accomplishments, the CDC was able to identify and control the type of bacteria that, in 1976, had caused a mysterious illness known as Legionnaire's Disease.

October 1918, twenty-one thousand Americans died from the flu. Philadelphia was particularly hard hit. Within a week after the first case of influenza was reported in that city, the disease had killed thirteen thousand people. New York City recorded 851 deaths in a single day, and, as in most other places, its toll kept rising. Doctors in almost every community had grim stories to tell. In Washington, D.C., a physician who had opened his own emergency hospital to care for flu victims said that "the only way we could find room for the sick was to have undertakers waiting at the door. . . . The living came in one door and the dead went out the other."

A great equalizer, the epidemic struck down the rich and famous as well as ordinary citizens. William Cody, better known as Buffalo Bill, the chief performer in his famous Wild West Show, lost both his daughter-in-law and his grandson to the flu. Katherine Anne Porter, destined to become one of America's most popular authors, nearly died of the disease. Her fiancé was killed in the epidemic. Later, in her short novel *Pale Horse, Pale Rider*, Porter would describe what her community was like during the time of the flu. "All the theaters and nearly all the shops and restaurants are closed," Porter would write, "and the streets have been full of funerals all day and ambulances all night."

By early 1919, about one in every four people in the United States had been stricken with the deadly disease. As the death toll mounted, Americans were filled with a terror few had ever experienced. Every day, it seemed another family member or another friend came down with the illness. Doctors and nurses throughout the nation worked around the clock because so many of their colleagues had also fallen victim. They did whatever they could to bring comfort to those who were ill. But they were powerless to bring a halt to a disease for which no cure had been found.

Desperate to find ways to stop the spread of the epidemic, public officials and private citizens tried everything they could think of. Everywhere, schools, churches, and places of amusement were ordered closed. Public funerals were banned. In some cities, signs were posted warning that anyone who was caught sneezing or coughing without using a handkerchief would be heavily fined or even imprisoned.

All types of cures were suggested. Some people tried eating huge amounts of garlic. Others took scalding baths, hoping they could sweat out any chance of falling ill. A few of the most desperate, having heard a rumor that this type of flu originated in the tonsils, had their tonsils removed.

The most common precaution was the wearing of face masks. In Tucson, Arizona, the board of health passed a law stating, "No person shall appear in any street, park, or place where any business is transacted or in

It was widely believed that wearing masks would prevent the spread of the deadly flu. Unfortunately, this was not true.

Culver Pictures

any other public place within the city of Tucson, without wearing a mask . . . covering both the nose and the mouth." Other cities soon followed Tucson's example. But the wearing of masks, the closing of public places, and the individual "cures" could not halt the flu from continuing to spread.

By the middle of 1919, nations around the world had been decimated. The number of dead was almost beyond belief. Mexico lost some five hundred thousand people. Four hundred fifty thousand Russians and more than two hundred twenty-eight thousand people in Great Britain lost their lives. The flu wiped out Eskimo villages in the Arctic and entire settlements in Central Africa. Densely populated India, where tens of millions lived closely huddled together, was the hardest hit of all. There, at least five million men, women, and children were killed by the disease.

Remarkably, the epidemic began to lose its grip almost as abruptly as it had begun. Even though the flu continued to claim victims well into 1920, by the end of that year the epidemic had run its course. In the United States, where more than five hundred thousand had died, as well as in the rest of the world, the grief that had been caused by the flu left little room for rejoicing.

What *is* to be celebrated is the fact that although influenza epidemics continue to occur every few years, advances in medicine have all but eliminated the possibility of a similar flu disaster from taking place again. Driven by the determination to prevent another such tragedy, scientists and medical researchers were finally able to identify the new virus that had caused the epidemic. They also discovered that the reason it was so deadly was that it damaged the lungs and made its victims extremely vulnerable to more serious bacterial infections. Armed with this knowledge, researchers then developed vaccines and antibiotics powerful enough either to prevent people from catching the flu or to reduce the severity of the illness if they did catch it.

It would be wonderful to end this story by saying that a cure has been found for all epidemics. But that is far from true. In the twenty-first century, millions of people worldwide are dying from a new terror known as AIDS (Acquired Immune Deficiency Syndrome).

So many people in the United States were struck down by influenza that hospitals simply could not accommodate all the victims. Like many communities, Lawrence, Massachusetts, was forced to care for many of its citizens in tents.

Culver Pictures

NASA

Death and destruction from earthquakes strike in many forms. One of
the greatest dangers exists in collapsed buildings and other structures.

EIGHT

EARTHQUAKES
The Restless Earth

One of the things that we take most for granted is the fact that the earth will remain solid and stable beneath our feet. When the earth begins to move violently and splits apart, those who are caught up in an earthquake experience a terror unlike any other.

Although it may be hard to believe, more than ten thousand earthquakes take place around the globe every year. Most are mild and go practically unnoticed. Some quakes are caused by the movement of the mixture of solid and liquid rock that lies under volcanoes. The most violent and most disastrous earthquakes, however, are those set into motion by movements that take place within the earth's "crust."

The crust is the layer of rock underneath the earth's soil. It contains many breaks, known as faults. The crust on either side of these faults moves very slowly. If two sections of crust become locked together and can't move, enormous pressure steadily mounts along that section of the fault. When the pressure is suddenly released by a shift of the crust on either side of the fault, it triggers a gigantic convulsion in the earth's surface, known as an earthquake.

The most devastating earthquake ever recorded took place in the Shaanxi Province of China in 1556. Many of the people in that area lived in caves and were buried by tons of rocks dislodged by the quake. More than eight hundred twenty-five thousand lost their lives.

Since that ancient catastrophe, millions of people around the world have been killed, seriously injured, or left homeless by violent earthquakes. Places such as Chimbote, Peru; Mexico City, Mexico; Valdivia, Chile; Spitak, Armenia; Tangshau, China; and Kobe, Japan have been decimated by quakes. In the year 2000 alone, earthquakes in El Salvador and India killed at least four hundred thousand people.

The United States has been free of such giant catastrophes—with one notable exception.

THE SAN FRANCISCO EARTHQUAKE

San Francisco, California, has been a city both blessed and cursed by its location. Perched on high hills overlooking the Pacific Ocean on one side and one of the world's loveliest harbors on the other, it is beautiful place to live.

It is also a city that grew almost overnight. At the start of 1848, San Francsico was a tiny village containing about thirty-five houses. Its number of residents was so small that, according to one visitor, "not more than twenty-five persons would be seen in the streets at any one time."

Then, on January 24, 1848, gold was discovered in the area. People everywhere dropped whatever they were doing and headed for the goldfields, hoping to strike it rich. Most made the long journey by ship, landing in San Francisco's wide harbor.

As millions of gold-seekers and thousands of merchants, anxious to sell supplies, poured into San Francisco, its population exploded. Even after the goldfields had been mined dry, tens of thousands who had fallen in love with the region remained and settled there. By 1906, the once-tiny village had become a booming city of more than four hundred thousand people.

By then it was a place with fine restaurants, luxurious hotels, and shipping facilities that attracted vessels from around the world. It was also a city that had become famous for the rich ethnic mix of its inhabitants, including Americans, Mexicans, Italians, Spaniards, and the largest settlement of Chinese in the nation.

But although few were aware of it at the time, the same physical location that had made San Francisco so attractive to its residents, its growing number of visitors, and its businessmen also placed everyone in the city in great danger. Unfortunately for San Francisco, the city had sprung up within a few miles of one of the greatest hidden earth fractures in the world. Known as the San Andreas Fault, this break in the earth's crust runs parallel to the California coastline for about 800 miles. By 1906, pressure had been building up along the fault near San Francisco for years. Early in the morning of April 18, 1906, all this pressure finally erupted and unleashed the greatest earthquake America has ever experienced.

The quake began out at sea, some ninety miles north of San Francisco. Traveling southward at an incredible two miles per second, it tore up the coastline in its path and headed directly toward the city. It hit San Francisco at 5:13 A.M.

A police sergeant named Jesse Cook was one of the first to witness the

TSUNAMIS: QUAKES BENEATH THE SEA

The San Francisco earthquake was the result of a severe break in the earth's crust. But there are other types of serious quakes called tsunamis that occur when there is a sudden collapse of a section of the ocean floor. When this happens, tons of water rush into the area where that section of the seafloor once was, setting the surrounding waters into motion. This creates waves that travel at speeds up to six hundred miles an hour toward the nearest shore. When these waves arrive at the shallower water of the coastline they suddenly rise to enormous heights.

When the huge waves of the tsunami crash upon the shore they can cause severe damage to coastal communities, particularly if they arrive without warning. In 1946, for example, a violent forty-foot wave from a tsunami crashed into the island of Hawaii, causing tens of millions of dollars in damage and killing 165 people.

Thankfully, today there are organizations such as the National Oceanographic and Atmospheric Administration's (NOAA) Pacific Marine Environmental Laboratory (PMEL). Aided by modern oceanographic equipment, such organizations are able to identify tsunamis almost at the moment they occur far out at sea. The instant warnings provided by such organizations have saved countless lives.

---

earthquake as it struck the city. "There was a deep rumble, deep and terrible, and then I could see it actually coming up Washington Street," remembered Cook. "The whole street was [moving up and down and splitting open]. It was as if the waves of the ocean were coming towards me, billowing as they came." Before Cook could react, he was sent flying by the violently moving earth, but he somehow managed to survive.

John Bartlett, the news editor of the San Francisco *Examiner* was standing on a street talking with two reporters when the quake hit. "Of a sudden," Bartlett later wrote, "we found ourselves staggering and reeling . . . then came the sickening sway of the earth that threw us flat upon our faces. . . . We could not get on our feet. I looked in a dazed fashion around me. . . . Big buildings were crumbling as one might crush a biscuit in one's hand. . . . Storms of masonry rained into the street. Wild, high jangles of smashing glass cut a sharp note into the frightful roaring. . . . Trolley tracks were twisted, their wires down, wriggling like serpents, flashing blue sparks all the time. . . . From the south of us, faint, but all too clear, came a horrible chorus of human cries of agony. Down there, in a ramshackle section of the city, the wretched houses had fallen in upon sleeping families. . . ."

Everywhere in the city, people lay dead or dying, crushed under the heavy wreckage of buildings and homes. Some of those who were not killed by the debris that pinned them down drowned in the tons of water pouring from broken water mains. For those who survived, it seemed as if the quake had gone on for more than an hour. Actually, it had lasted little more than a minute.

As if the quake itself had not been catastrophic enough, another horror lay immediately ahead. Within half an hour of the earthquake, more than fifty major fires erupted throughout the already devastated city. Many were caused by gas mains and live electric cables that had been broken by the quake. Others were caused by hot coals that had spilled out of woodstoves in homes and offices throughout San Francisco. By early afternoon, the entire downtown district of the city was on fire. So too was the waterfront. In the end, the death and destruction from all these fires would be far greater than the toll taken by the trembling earth and the toppling buildings.

One of the reasons that the fires were so devastating was the material

Sightseers have always been drawn to the scene of disasters. These people, perched on a hill above San Francisco, were eyewitnesses to the country's most disastrous earthquake.

used to construct San Francisco's homes, public buildings, and warehouses. Most of them were made of wood, crowded together, allowing the fire to spread quickly from building to building. For years, San Francisco fire chief Dennis Sullivan had been warning that more money should be spent on fire-fighting equipment in order to prevent such a disaster. But city officials had ignored his pleas.

By the time the city's undermanned and underequipped fire department was finally able to respond to the conflagrations, the fires were spreading to every corner of the city.

Battling such an inferno was challenging enough, but San Francisco's firemen were without their leader at a time when they most needed his skill and experience. When the quake had struck, Fire Chief Sullivan had been asleep in a fire station. Awakened by the sound of falling bricks, he had raced in the dark to rescue his wife from their apartment, which was above the station. Blinded by mortar dust, he was unaware that the floor of their bedroom and the bedrooms beneath it had collapsed in the quake. Entering the room, Sullivan fell through the opening and plunged three floors below to his death.

Still, San Francisco's firefighters fought valiantly to put out the flames. In one important area of the city—the waterfront—they were successful. There, by pouring water from the bay directly on the fires and with the help of navy fireboats, they were able to save the warehouses and other buildings that were vital to San Francisco's economy.

But the fires within the city itself could not be controlled. With so many water mains broken and with the pipes leading from the city's reservoirs destroyed by the quake, there simply was not enough water to fight the fires.

Desperate city officials felt they had no choice but to call in the army. Troops began to blow up buildings in order to create gaps between the structures that would be too wide for the flames to cross. It might have

"When the quake was over, we could hardly believe our eyes. Houses tilted crazily. Much of the city was reduced to rubble."
—*San Francisco resident*

been a good idea, but the hastily assembled army troops had no experience in creating firebreaks with explosives. In instance after instance, they indiscriminately blew up buildings, causing far more harm than good. San Francisco's Chinatown, for example, which had miraculously remained almost free of fires, was set fully ablaze by explosives set off by the troops.

With firefighters looking on helplessly, the fires were allowed to rage on for three days. Finally they burned themselves out. When they were over, two-thirds of San Francisco had been destroyed and its central business district was completely demolished. The human toll was even more devastating. Although the exact figure would never be known, at least eight hundred people were killed and more than four hundred were seriously injured.

San Francisco's once-vibrant Chinatown district was one of the areas most heavily damaged by the earthquake and the ensuing fires.

Following the earthquake, after-shocks rocked the city for days. Those lucky citizens who had not lost their homes were afraid to return to their dwellings. Many took to preparing their meals in the street.

The vast majority of those who had died were victims of the fires rather than the earthquake itself.

Widespread looting took place amid the confusion of the quake and the fires. Army troops were instructed to shoot looters on sight. Among their victims were several unfortunate innocent people who were picking through their own destroyed homes looking for treasured possessions.

Once again, as in previous great tragedies, both the government and private citizens responded generously to the disaster. Tens of millions of dollars were donated to aid quake victims and to finance the rebuilding of the city. Dozens of supply trains poured into San Francisco filled with medicine, food, clothing, and building materials. The Red Cross and other agencies set up scores of tents, out of which they fed the hungry. The army erected eight thousand long wooden barracks to house those who had lost their homes.

For their own part, the people of San Francisco responded to the catastrophe with courage and determination. Within a year, almost all of the wreckage caused by the quake had been removed. Within three years, more than twenty thousand new homes and buildings had been erected, and thousands of others were under construction. In 1915 an almost totally rebuilt San Francisco hosted a gigantic world's fair.

Today, San Francisco is one of the nation's most vibrant cities. Thanks to lessons learned from the 1906 quake, it has one of the strictest building codes in the world. Its architects continue to seek new construction methods and new building materials designed to make the city's structures as earthquake-proof as possible. But one thing cannot be changed: San Francisco still lies next to the San Andreas Fault. As one earth scientist has warned, "the further you are from the last big earthquake, the nearer you are to the next."

Volcanoes present an ongoing danger to all those who live in their vicinity.
Scientists, filmmakers, and photographers study and record them
constantly in an effort to predict their next eruptions.

VOLCANOES
Danger from Beneath the Earth

Volcanoes are among the most fascinating of all natural phenomena. Usually located along ocean ridges, they are formed when melted rock (called magma) and dissolved gases from deep within the earth make their way to the surface and escape through an opening in the earth's crust. There are three different kinds of volcanic openings, each resulting in a different type of volcanic eruption.

Hot spot volcanoes are formed when an upward rush of magma (called lava when it reaches the earth's surface) suddenly breaks through the earth's crust at one particular spot. Rift volcanoes are formed when magma regularly flows to the surface in a particular area. Since most rift volcanoes are located on the ocean floor, they go largely unnoticed. The most devastating of all volcanoes are called subduction volcanoes. They occur when two plates beneath the earth (usually on the ocean floor) collide. The collision causes the extraordinarily hot magma to rise and become trapped in the earth's crust until it explodes violently into the air.

Volcanic eruptions provide spectacular sights, but they are often deadly. A volcanic eruption produces devastating lava flows as well as pyroclastic flows. Pyroclastic flows, made of rock fragments, race across the ground at a hundred miles an hour, accompanied by huge explosions. They can hurl huge chunks of rocks (lava bombs), spew tons of ash into the air, trigger avalanches of debris and mud slides, and cause forest fires.

The most famous of all volcanic disasters took place in A.D. 79 when Italy's Mount Vesuvius erupted. Three Roman towns—Stabiae, Herculaneum, and Pompeii—were buried in ash, killing sixteen thousand people. The Mount Vesuvius tragedy has become the most storied of all eruptions. But there have been others that have been far more devastating.

In 1883, one of the volcanoes in the small Indonesian island of Krakatau erupted, triggering ocean storms with waves more than 130 feet high. The waves swept over the coastlines of Java and Sumatra, killing more than thirty-six thousand men, women, and children. In 1902, thirty thousand residents of St. Pierre, Martinique, perished when Mount Pelée on that West Indian island erupted. In 1985, twenty-one thousand residents of Amero, Colombia, died when they were buried in enormous mud slides caused by the eruption of Nevado del Ruiz.

The United States was spared a volcanic disaster until late in the twentieth century. No person in the contiguous United States had ever been killed in a volcanic eruption until May 1980. In that month, the people of the Pacific Northwest learned just how dangerous a volcano can be.

THE MOUNT ST. HELENS ERUPTION

Over the years, the greatest amount of volcanic activity within the United States has taken place in the Cascade Mountains. The Cascades run along the Pacific Coast of Canada and the United States, extending south from British Columbia to northern California. The range contains fifteen volcanoes. All the majestic peaks of its mountains are the result of lava and other debris from volcanic eruptions that began millions of years ago.

Mount St. Helens is located in the southwest corner of Washington State. The mountain, named for an eighteenth-century diplomat, last erupted in 1857. No one was killed but, according to the Native Americans who lived near the mountain, the eruption caused a woman named Loo-wit to be turned into Mount St. Helens's beautiful, snow-capped peak to provide fire to the Great Spirit.

By 1980, Mount St. Helens had long been one of the nation's favorite destinations for tourists and vacationers. Its distinctive conical shape and symmetrical, snow-covered peak had earned it the nickname "the Mount Fuji of America." The area around the mountain was as lovely as the mountain itself. The streams in the region were filled with salmon and trout. Black-tailed deer, elk, and mountain lions roamed through the area's forests. The region was a nature lover's paradise. But not everyone was sure that the paradise would last forever.

As early as the 1950s, two United States Geological Survey (USGS) scientists began studying Mount St. Helens. They were concerned about the fact that the volcanic mountain was only forty-five miles from the heavily populated Portland / Vancouver area. Even though they knew that the mountain had not erupted in nearly a hundred years, they also knew that a new eruption would be disastrous. In 1978 other scientists warned the

VOLCANOLOGY: A HOT SCIENCE

The large number of volcanic eruptions that have occurred has led to a relatively new field of scientific endeavor known as volcanology. Volcanologists study the many geological factors that lead to volcanic eruptions. They also study distant and recent history of a particular volcano to find clues as to if and when the volcano is likely to erupt again. And when a volcano does come to life, volcanologists arrive on the scene to monitor its activity, aid officials in establishing evacuation plans, and develop strategies to safeguard the public.

Volcanology is often a dangerous profession, particularly for those scientists whose work takes them into the mouth of potential or ongoing eruptions. David Johnston and his colleagues who were killed in the Mount St. Helens disaster were not the only volcanologists to die in the line of duty. In 1991, for example, French volcanologists Maurice and Katia Krafft and American scientist Harry Elicken lost their lives during the eruption of Japan's Mount Unzen. In January 1993, six scientists who were installing monitoring equipment at the Galeras volcano in Colombia were killed when it suddenly erupted.

Yet despite the dangers, volcanologists around the world continue to pursue their endeavors. Motivated by the human benefit their work brings, most remain determined to monitor volcanic activity, educate the public about the nature of volcanoes, and develop new and better techniques that will make forecasting an eruption a more precise science.

public that Mount St. Helens needed to be watched closely.

Beginning on March 20, 1980, their warning came true. First, a series of moderate earthquakes shook the area around the mountain. Exactly one week later, an even more dramatic event occurred when a huge noise was heard and a cloud of smoke and debris suddenly rose sixty-five hundred feet above the volcano. The eruption had opened a crater north of the mountain's summit.

The eruption caught the attention of both the public and of earth scientists who had ignored the earlier warnings about the volcano. Teams of earth scientists, mostly from the USGS, descended upon the area, bringing with them all types of modern volcano-monitoring devices that they set up at various places on the mountain.

One of the scientists, David Johnston, had already been studying the volcano from a 4,500-foot-high observation post near the mountain. As a result of his observations, he was convinced that the eruption that had taken place was a prelude to a much bigger blast. "This is an extremely dangerous place to be," Johnston told a reporter for an Oregon newspaper. "If it were to erupt right now, we would die. We're standing next to a dynamite keg and the fuse is lit. We just don't know how long the fuse is."

Other scientists, however, disagreed with Johnston. One of his supervisors told the same newspaper reporter that a further eruption would send out only a small blanket of ash.

During the three weeks after Johnston's observations other small eruptions took place that opened up a secondary crater at the top of the mountain. By mid-April the two craters had formed a single crater four hundred yards across.

But concern over this development was minor compared to that which was felt when a huge bulge suddenly appeared on Mount St. Helens's north side. Even more ominous, the bulge immediately began to grow at an alarming rate. By early May it extended more than three hundred feet northward and was becoming six feet larger every day.

At this point, Washington Governor Dixy Lee Ray set up a "red zone" radiating five miles around the mountain. People living or working within the zone were ordered to evacuate the area, and all roads leading into it were closed. The mandatory evacuation was met with complaints from residents in the area and from sight-seers anxious to get as close to the mountain as possible. Nevertheless, the zone emptied of almost all residents.

By this time rumblings inside the volcano that had been heard for months had grown considerably louder. Yet, despite the rumblings, the ever-growing bulge, and the fact that Mount St. Helens had become the most closely monitored volcano in history, people were still surprised when it finally blew its top. And, perhaps with the exception of David Johnston, no one had any inkling that the eruption would be so catastrophic.

On Sunday, May 18, residents and tourists in the Mount St. Helens area awoke to a clear, beautiful morning. At the USGS headquarters in Vancouver, scientists were beginning another day of monitoring the volcano. At 8:32 A.M., David Johnston reported by radio from his position five and a half miles from the mountain. "Vancouver! Vancouver! This is it," the volcanologist shouted. At the same time, a volunteer radio operator named Gerald Martin screamed into his own transmitter: "The whole north side [of the mountain] is giving way. It's consuming the USGS people [other scientists who were with Johnston] and it's going to get me."

He was right. Within two minutes of their reports, David Johnston and his colleagues would be dead. For what they had witnessed was Mount St. Helens exploding with a force far greater than that any nuclear bomb had ever made.

The incredible blast blew off the entire north side of Mount St. Helens, sending enormous clouds of burning ash as high as fifteen miles into the sky. Poisonous gas, along with the ash, was sent racing across the landscape at speeds of up to 180 miles per hour. As the mountain collapsed, it triggered one of the greatest landslides in history. Some two hundred fifty square miles of forests containing more than 6 million mature trees were leveled in an instant. All forms of wildlife within a fan-shaped seventeen-mile-long area were killed. The avalanche also choked the area's Spirit Lake and the Toutle and Cowlitz rivers with huge boulders and other debris, setting off record-breaking floods.

Amazingly, some people in the blast zone survived the eruption. The U.S. Forest Service's Krau Kilpatrick was planting trees some three miles down the south side of the mountain. "There was no sound to it, not a sound," Kilpatrick later reported. "It was like a silent movie and we were all in it. First the ash cloud shot out to the east, then to the west, then some lighter stuff started shooting straight up. . . . I could see boulders being hurled out of the leading edge, and then being swept up again in the advancing cloud."

As unforgettable as the explosion was, what most people outside the blast zone may remember most was the ash that blanketed their communities for days. Fanned by the wind, the ash spread east and came down like a blizzard on eastern Washington, northwest Oregon, Idaho, and western Montana.

Before the devastating May 18, 1980, eruption, Mount St. Helens was regarded as one of the most beautiful and most frequently climbed peaks in the Cascade Range. Spirit Lake, at the foot of the mountain, also attracted many vacationers.

U.S. Geological Survey

After the initial eruption on May 18, 1980, five volcanic explosions rocked Mount St. Helens. The enormous clouds of smoke and ash could be seen a hundred miles away.

In many communities, some as far as 85 miles away from the volcano, day turned into night as the ash completely blocked out the sun.

Almost all normal life in these areas was brought to a halt. Roads, covered with up to three inches of the white, talcumlike powder, were closed for days. People wore masks to protect themselves from inhaling the powder. Wherever it fell, the ash clogged engines of every type. Automobiles refused to start, and in Washington more than half of the state-police cars were out of commission.

But, for the most part, these were inconveniences compared to the real toll of the eruption. In addition to the forests, homes, buildings, roads, and bridges that were destroyed in the disaster, agriculture in the region was also dealt a heavy blow. Fruit crops were severely damaged, the hay harvest was destroyed, and millions of Chinook salmon and steelhead trout, for which the area was famous, were killed in the region's overheated rivers and streams.

The beauty of Mount St. Helens also was a victim of the disaster. Gone was the celebrated conical peak, replaced by an enormous gaping hole. The blast had reduced the height of the mountain from more than 9,600 feet to its present height of 8,363 feet.

Most serious of all was the loss of human life. Although official reports contradict each other, at least sixty-two people were killed by the force of the blast and the onslaught of falling trees, ash, and mud.

Tragic as this loss of life was, however, it was much smaller compared with dozens of other less explosive volcanic eruptions. Fortunately, the immediate area around the mountain was sparsely inhabited. Governor Ray's evacuation order had also removed many would-be victims from the vicinity. And since the eruption took place on a Sunday, none of the hundreds of lumberjacks were at work in the forests that had been decimated.

In the years immediately following the Mount St. Helens disaster, nature once again provided concrete reminders of its resiliency. Scores of types of vegetation began to reappear in the stricken region. Within three years of the eruption that had laid waste to so large an area, 90 percent of the native plant species reappeared. Elk, bears, cougars, and other wildlife also began to return.

Perhaps the positive effects of the disaster were the lessons learned from the event. Mount St. Helens had provided scientists an unprecedented opportunity to study a volcano that was about to erupt and to develop and improve techniques for predicting future eruptions. It was a lesson well

Volcanologists and other scientists are determined that the 1980 Mount St. Helens disaster will not be repeated. They monitor the mountain constantly for signs of eruption.

learned. Almost all of the twenty-four eruptions that took place in the seven years following the calamity were accurately predicted. Motivated by the Mount St. Helens experience, scientists in both the public and private sectors have devoted themselves to developing the most advanced volcano-predicting equipment and methods possible. And the public has learned that evacuation warnings are not to be taken lightly.

Today, the Mount St. Helens area is a designated National Volcanic Monument. Perhaps the mountain's greatest legacy is the fact that the United States government now uses the site to educate people about the dangers of volcanic eruptions.

FURTHER READING

There is not enough space for me to list all of the books, magazines articles, newspaper reports, and other materials that were vital to the research I conducted for *America's Great Disasters*. Listed below, however, are books that have been particularly helpful to me and also make good and useful reading for anyone interested in fascinating stories of disasters and what we can learn from them. I've divided my list into two categories—general books on disasters and books dealing specifically with disasters I've included in this volume.

GENERAL BOOKS ON DISASTERS

Catastrophe and Crisis by Jeremy Kingston and David Lambert (New York: Facts on File, 1979).

Dangerous Weather by Michael Allaby (New York: Facts on File, 1988).

Devastation: The World's Worst Natural Disasters by Lesley Newson (New York: DK Publishing, 1998).

Disaster: Major American Catastrophes by A. A. Hoehling (New York: Hawthorn Books, 1973).

Disasters That Shook the World by Cathie Cush (Austin, Texas: Steck Vaughn, 1993).

Fire on the Rim by Stephen J. Pyne (Seattle: University of Washington Press, 1995).

Great Disasters: Dramatic True Stories of Nature's Awesome Powers by the Editors of *Reader's Digest* (Pleasantville, New York: Reader's Digest Association, 1989).

Great Ship Disasters by A. A. Hoehling (New York: Cowles, 1971).

Historical Catastrophes: Fires by Walter R. Brown and Norman D. Anderson (Reading, Massachusetts: Addison-Wesley, 1975).

Historical Catastrophes: Floods by Walter R. Brown and Norman D. Anderson (Reading, Massachusetts: Addison-Wesley, 1975).

Historical Catastrophes: Snowstorms and Avalanches by Walter R. Brown and Norman D. Anderson (Reading, Massachusetts: Addison-Wesley, 1975).

Natural Disasters by the Editors of *Reader's Digest* (London; New York: Reader's Digest, 1997).

Quakes, Eruptions, and Other Geologic Cataclysms by Jon Erickson, Alexander E. Gates (New York: Facts on File, 2001).

SPECIFIC DISASTERS

The *Sultana*

The following books contain the most complete accounts written about the *Sultana* disaster. They are each filled with anecdotes and firsthand accounts and use a good deal of material from an early book written about the *Sultana* tragedy, *Loss of the* Sultana *and Reminiscences of Survivors* by Chester D. Berry (Lansing, Michigan: Darius D. Thorp, 1892).

Disaster on the Mississippi by Gene Eric Salecker (Annapolis, Maryland: Naval Institute Press, 1996).

The Sultana Tragedy by Jerry O. Potter (Gretna, Louisiana: Pelican Publishing Co., 1992).

The Johnstown Flood

These three books contain detailed descriptions of the Johnstown flood. They are filled with scores of pictures and firsthand accounts.

The Great Flood by Anwei Skinses Law (Johnstown, Pennsylvania: Johnstown Area Heritage Association, 1997).

The Johnstown Flood by David McCullough (New York: Simon & Schuster, 1987).

The Johnstown Flood of 1889 by Paula and Carl Degen (Washington, D.C.: Eastern National, 2000).

The Dust Bowl

The following two books are filled with dramatic photographs depicting the many aspects of the Dust Bowl disaster.

In This Proud Land by Roy Emerson Stryker and Nancy Wood (New York: Galahad Books, 1973).

Photographs of a Lifetime by Dorothea Lange (New York: Aperture, 1982).

The Wisconsin Forest Fire

This book contains vivid descriptions and eyewitness accounts of America's most disastrous forest fire.

The Great Peshtigo Fire by Peter Pernin (Madison, Wisconsin: University of Wisconsin Press, 1999).

The Galveston Hurricane

These two books provide the most complete and interesting accounts of America's most disastrous hurricane.

Isaac's Storm by Erik Larson (New York: Crown Publishers, 1999).

Through a Night of Horrors edited by Casey Edward Greene and Shelly Henley Kelly (College Station, Texas: Texas A&M University Press, 2000).

The Blizzard of '88

This book, which covers several weather-related disasters, contains an excellent account of the blizzard of '88.

Killer Weather by Howard Everett Smith (New York: Dodd, Mead, 1982).

The Flu Epidemic of 1918–19

The following books provide highly readable, fascinating accounts of the flu epidemic of 1918–19 and scientists' efforts to understand the flu virus.

America's Forgotten Pandemic by Alfred W. Crosby (New York: Cambridge University Press, 1990).

Flu: The Story of the Great Influenza Pandemic of 1918 and the Search for the Virus That Caused It by Gina Kolata (New York: Farrar, Straus & Giroux, 1999).

The San Francisco Earthquake

This book is filled with fascinating facts and eyewitness accounts of the United States's most devastating quake to date.

The San Francisco Earthquake by Gordon Thomas and Max Morgan Witts (New York: Stein and Day, 1995).

Mount St. Helens

The following three books provide excellent reading on the disastrous Mt. St. Helens eruption.

Earthfire: The Eruption of Mount St. Helens by Charles Rosenfeld and Robert Cooke (Cambridge, Massachusetts: MIT Press, 1982).

Mount St. Helens: A Sleeping Volcano Awakes by Marian T. Place (New York: Dodd, Mead, 1981).

The Mount St. Helens Disaster: What We've Learned by Thomas G. and Virginia L. Aylesworth (New York: Franklin Watts 1983).

You are a child of the universe,
No less than the trees and stars;
You have a right to be here.
And whether or not it is clear to you,
No doubt the universe is unfolding as it should.

—Max Ehrmann

BELOVED DEVIN
OCTOBER 27, 1964 - MARCH 17, 2000

The Devin Shafron Memorial Book Fund